WHALES SET II

DWARF SPERM WHALES

Kristin Petrie
ABDO Publishing Company

visit us at
www.abdopub.com

Published by ABDO Publishing Company, 4940 Viking Drive, Edina, Minnesota 55435.
Copyright © 2006 by Abdo Consulting Group, Inc. International copyrights reserved in all
countries. No part of this book may be reproduced in any form without written permission from
the publisher. The Checkerboard Library™ is a trademark and logo of ABDO Publishing
Company.

Printed in the United States.

Cover Photo: © Robert L. Pitman / SeaPics.com
Interior Photos: © Benjamin Kahn / SeaPics.com p. 18; © David B. Fleetham / SeaPics.com
    p. 17; © Doug Perrine / SeaPics.com p. 21; © Jeff Rotman / SeaPics.com p. 12;
    © Michael S. Nolan / SeaPics.com pp. 11, 15; © Robert L. Pitman / SeaPics.com pp. 5, 19;
    © Romeo /V&W/ SeaPics.com p. 13; Uko Gorter pp. 6-7

Series Coordinator: Stephanie Hedlund
Editors: Tamara L. Britton, Stephanie Hedlund
Art Direction & Maps: Neil Klinepier

Library of Congress Cataloging-in-Publication Data

Petrie, Kristin, 1970-
    Dwarf sperm whales / Kristin Petrie.
        p. cm. -- (Whales. Set II)
    ISBN 1-59679-308-2
    1. Dwarf sperm whale--Juvenile literature. I. Title.

QL737.C435P48 2005
599.5'47--dc22
                                                            2005043336

CONTENTS

DWARF SPERM WHALES AND FAMILY

Whales are some of the largest animals in the world. They live in salty ocean water that supports their weight. This is why they are able to grow to such a large size.

Whales are mammals. They belong to the order **Cetacea**. In this order, there are three divisions. Dwarf sperm whales belong to the toothed whales, or Odontoceti group. There are about 70 species in this group, including the *Kogia simus*.

Of all the whale species the *Kogia simus*, or dwarf sperm whale, is the smallest. Dwarf sperm whales were discovered in 1866. But, they have been difficult to study. They live far from the shore and are rarely seen. This is partly due to their quiet nature.

For these reasons, much about dwarf sperm whales is a mystery to humans. But, **stranded** animals provide information that shows they should be set apart. In 1966, they were finally declared an individual species.

Dwarf sperm whales are often confused with other marine animals. They may be mistaken for the pygmy sperm whale or some shark species.

SHAPE, SIZE, AND COLOR

Dwarf sperm whales are small. The average dwarf sperm whale is 7 to 11 feet (2 to 3 m) long. But, it still weighs in at 300 to 600 pounds (135 to 270 kg)! So much weight on a small frame gives this whale a robust body.

The whale's boxy head starts with a slightly pointed snout. The dwarf sperm whale's head

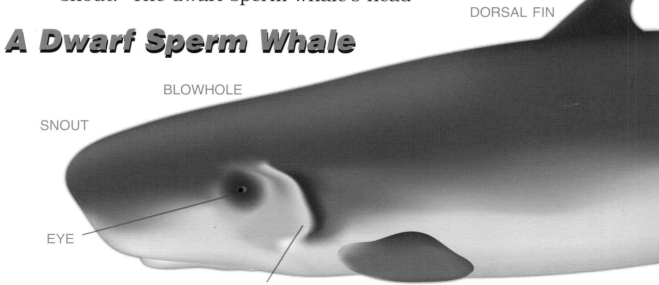

A Dwarf Sperm Whale

DORSAL FIN

BLOWHOLE

SNOUT

EYE

FALSE GILL

FLIPPER

changes shape with age. Older whales have blunter, squarer heads.

The dwarf sperm whale has several other unusual features. Its lower jaw sprouts long, sharp teeth. Its blowhole is slightly to the left. There is also a light marking called a false gill behind each eye.

The dwarf sperm whale's **dorsal** fin is wide with a pointy tip. The flukes, or tail fins, are also wide with sharp points. The flippers are more like paddles. They are broad, with rounded edges.

Dwarf sperm whales are bluish gray or dark gray to black. Their bellies are lighter gray or white. This delicate underside is sometimes a speckled pink.

FLUKE

WHERE THEY LIVE

Dwarf sperm whales prefer **temperate** and tropical regions. They are found in the Atlantic, Pacific, and Indian oceans.

They are also seen in the gulfs of California and Mexico. There, they have been spotted close to shore. The **continental shelf** is a popular hangout.

Usually, dwarf sperm whales stick to deep waters of about 985 feet (300 m). However, the stomachs of **stranded** dwarf sperm whales have revealed they may feed deeper. These specimens contained food that lives between 1,640 and 4,265 feet (500 and 1,300 m) deep.

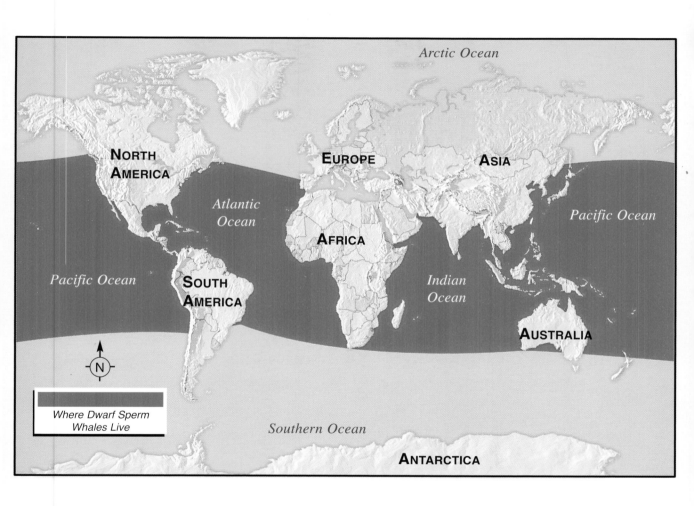

Arctic Ocean

NORTH
AMERICA

EUROPE

ASIA

Atlantic
Ocean

Pacific Ocean

Pacific Ocean

AFRICA

SOUTH
AMERICA

Indian
Ocean

AUSTRALIA

N

Where Dwarf Sperm
Whales Live

Southern Ocean

ANTARCTICA

SENSES

Like all whales, dwarf sperm whales have little or no sense of smell. They rely on vision and hearing to get around their **habitat**.

The dwarf sperm whale also has the spermaceti **organ** that is found in sperm whales. Some believe this organ is used to focus the signals used in echolocation.

Most whales and some other mammals use echolocation. This is when they send out sounds to provide information about their surroundings. Noise from a whale's throat travels through the ocean water. It bounces off objects and returns to the whale.

The echoing noise provides all kinds of information. For example, a noise may bounce off an approaching ship. This tells the whale to get out of the way. Another noise could bounce off a squid. What does this tell the whale? That it's lunchtime!

Toothed whales have an organ called a melon in the front of their head. This feature, along with the spermaceti organ, helps the dwarf sperm whale to focus the signals echolocation provides.

DEFENSE

The dwarf sperm whale faces the same dangers as other sea life. These dangers include natural **predators**, such as large sharks and killer whales.

If a dwarf sperm whale is frightened, it may **secrete** a red liquid. This causes a cloud to form that stops or distracts predators. This allows the whale to dive deep into the ocean and escape.

Threats from humans are also a concern to this mammal's well-being. Large fishing nets and pollution are this whale's

The dwarf sperm whale's secretion defense works much like that of this giant Pacific octopus.

Fishing nets are also a threat to the large sperm whale.

greatest threats. Dwarf sperm whales were never hunted in great numbers. More often, they were sold at market after accidental catches.

Today, a small amount of dwarf sperm whaling occurs near Japan's southern coast and Indonesia. But, it is not known how many of these whales are out there. The good news is that the world's smallest whale appears to be more common than previously believed.

FOOD

One of the dwarf sperm whale's favorite prey is squid. These whales dive to great depths for this tasty meal. Dwarf sperm whales also feed on an assortment of fish and **crustaceans**.

Unfortunately, dwarf sperm whales are slow creatures. They move much, much slower than their prey. Therefore, hunting is done by **stealth**.

Dwarf sperm whales have 14 to 26 sharp, curved teeth in their lower jaw. These come in handy for catching quick prey. Six smaller, nonworking teeth are in the upper jaw.

Even with all those teeth, dwarf sperm whales eat their food whole. Like other whales, their stomachs have several chambers. This allows them to **digest** their food without chewing!

The dwarf sperm whale's teeth are similar to this sperm whale's. But, the sperm whale has 40 to 52 teeth. That is more than twice the amount of the dwarf sperm whale.

Babies

Dwarf sperm whales begin reproducing when they are about six feet (2 m) long. The female dwarf sperm whale is **pregnant** for 9 to 11 months. After this period, a small whale is born. Baby dwarf sperm whales, called calves, are usually born in the winter.

A dwarf sperm calf is often three feet (1 m) long. Female dwarf sperm whales nurse their calves with milk. Mother and calf stick together for a long time, possibly a year. That may be because many female dwarf sperm whales give birth every year.

Whales live in groups called pods. Dwarf sperm pods of up to ten members have been sighted. These pods often include mature females and their calves, along with immature whales.

Like this pod of pygmy sperm whales, dwarf sperm whales live in small groups.

BEHAVIORS

Dwarf sperm whales have been seen in pods for feeding and mating. However, grown-up dwarf sperm whales often spend their time alone or in pairs.

Lying motionless at the surface is called logging. This may be how whales sleep.

These whales are slow swimmers. When it is time to dive, they simply drop below the surface. They may dive as deep as 985 feet (300 m). Occasionally, the dwarf sperm whale will breach, or jump out of the water and land in a belly flop.

Usually, dwarf sperm whales lie motionless at the water's surface. Their **blow** is low, and they tend to avoid ships and humans. For these reasons, they are not easily identified by whale watchers.

Instead, dwarf sperm whales are studied after **stranding**. Some whales are rushed to aquariums and saved. Others make it back to the ocean with the high tide. Still others die on the shore.

Sperm whales are known for mass stranding, or having three or more whales strand at one time.

DWARF SPERM WHALE FACTS

Scientific Name: *Kogia simus*

Common Name: Dwarf Sperm Whale

Other Names: Owen's Pygmy Sperm Whale

Average Size:
Length - 7 to 11 feet (2 to 3 m)
Weight - 300 to 600 pounds (135 to 270 kg)

Where They Are Found: Atlantic, Pacific, and Indian oceans and the gulfs of California and Mexico

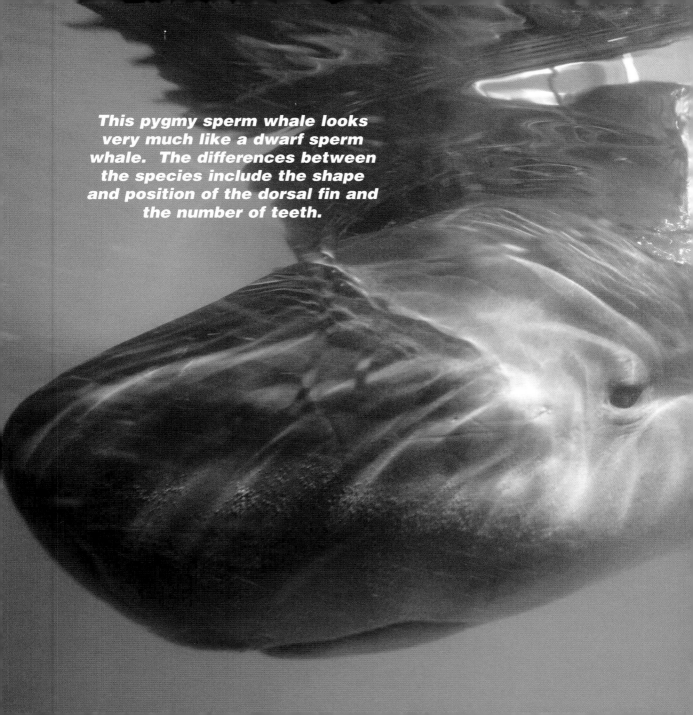

This pygmy sperm whale looks very much like a dwarf sperm whale. The differences between the species include the shape and position of the dorsal fin and the number of teeth.

GLOSSARY

blow - a mix of air and water droplets that are released when a marine mammal breathes.

Cetacea - an order of mammal, such as the whale, that lives in the water like fish. Members of this order are called cetaceans.

continental shelf - a shallow, underwater plain that borders a continent and ends with a steep slope to the ocean floor.

crustacean (kruhs-TAY-shuhn) - any of a group of animals with hard shells that live mostly in water. Crabs, lobsters, and shrimps are all crustaceans.

digest - to break down food into substances small enough for the body to absorb.

dorsal - located near or on the back, especially of an animal.

habitat - a place where a living thing is naturally found.

organ - a part of an animal or plant that is composed of several kinds of tissues and that performs a specific function. The heart, liver, gallbladder, and intestines are organs of an animal.

predator - an animal that kills and eats other animals.

pregnant - having one or more babies growing within the body.

secrete - to form and give off.

stealth - an action or behavior performed in a secretive or sneaky manner.

stranding - the appearance of a cetacean on a beach. Without help from humans, a stranded whale often dies.

temperate - having neither very hot nor very cold weather.

WEB SITES

To learn more about dwarf sperm whales, visit ABDO Publishing Company on the World Wide Web at **www.abdopub.com**. Web sites about these whales are featured on our Book Links page. These links are routinely monitored and updated to provide the most current information available.

INDEX